# I LOVE NEW YORK

## ABOUT "GOD BLESS AMERICA"

"GOD BLESS AMERICA" by Irving Berlin was first published in 1938. Almost as soon as the song began generating revenue, Mr. Berlin established The God Bless America Fund to benefit American youth.

Over $7,000,000 has been distributed to date, primarily to two youth organizations with which Mr. and Mrs. Berlin were personally involved: the Girl Scout Council of Greater New York, and the Greater New York Councils of the Boy Scouts of America. These councils do not discriminate on any basis and are committed to serving all segments of New York City's diverse youth population.

The trustees of The God Bless America Fund are working with the two councils to ensure that funding is allocated for New York City children affected by the tragic events of September 11, 2001.

ISBN 0-634-04615-2

GOD BLESS AMERICA is a registered trademark of the Trustees of the God Bless America Fund.

## HAL·LEONARD® CORPORATION

7777 W. BLUEMOUND RD. P.O. BOX 13819 MILWAUKEE, WI 53213

Visit Hal Leonard Online at
**www.halleonard.com**

# CONTENTS

# AUTUMN IN NEW YORK

Words and Music by
VERNON DUKE

# BROADWAY BABY
## from FOLLIES

Words and Music by
STEPHEN SONDHEIM

D.S. al Coda

plus a tube of grease - paint and a fol - low spot!___ I'm a

**CODA**

I can get to strut my stuff,___

work - ing for a nice man like a Zieg - feld or a Weiss - man in a big - time

Broad - way show!___

# THE BOY FROM NEW YORK CITY

Words and Music by JOHN TAYLOR
and GEORGE DAVIS

**Moderate and very steady**

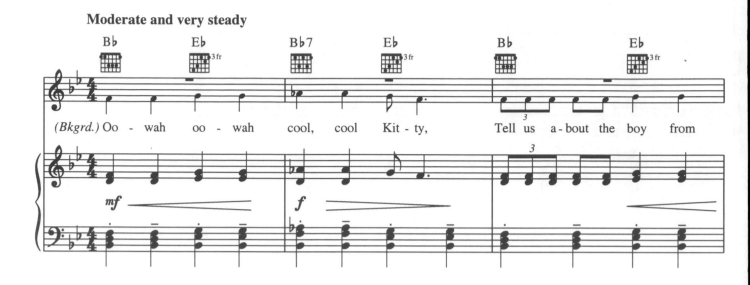

(Bkgrd.) Oo - wah oo - wah cool, cool Kit - ty, Tell us a - bout the boy from

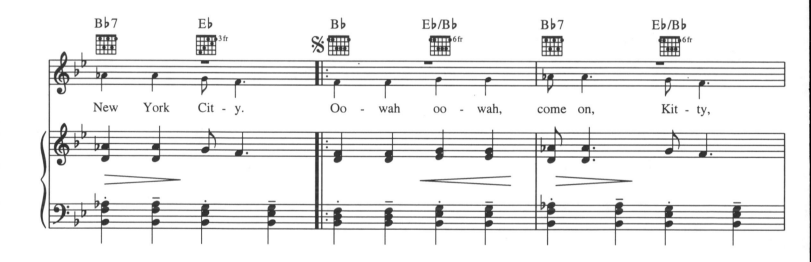

New York Cit - y. Oo - wah oo - wah, come on, Kit - ty,

Tell us a - bout the boy from New York Cit - y.
1. He's kind - a    tall. _____
2. He's real - ly   down, _____
3.      He can   dance. _____

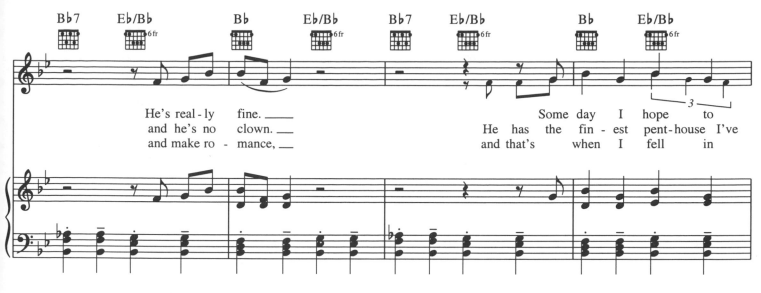

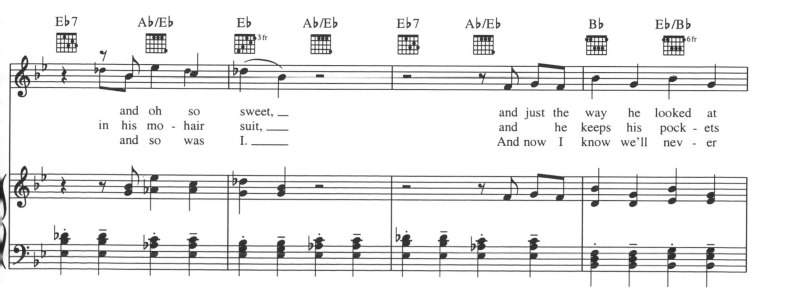

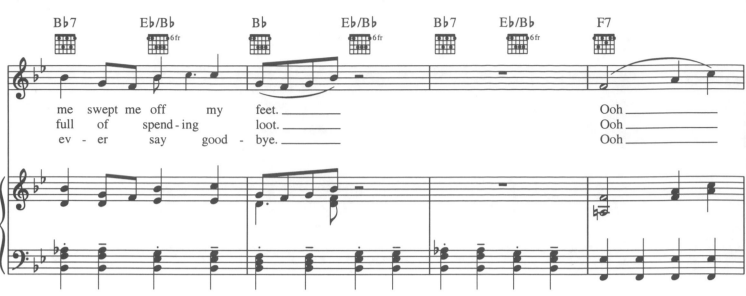

me swept me off my feet. _____ Ooh _____
full of spend-ing loot. _____ Ooh _____
ev - er say good - bye. _____ Ooh _____

ee, _____ you ought to come and see _____ how he
ee, _____ you ought to come and see _____ his pret - ty
ee, _____ you ought to come and see, _____ he's the

To Coda

walks, ___ and how he talks. ___
bar, ___ and his brand new car. ___
most ___ from coast to coast. ___

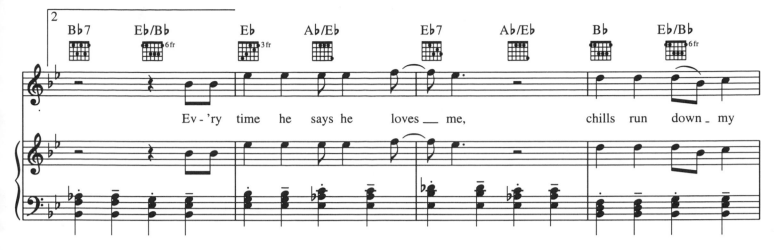

Ev-'ry time he says he loves __ me, chills run down __ my

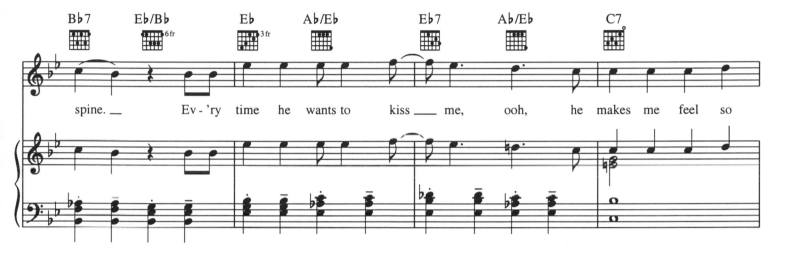

spine. __ Ev-'ry time he wants to kiss __ me, ooh, he makes me feel so

fine, __ yeah! __

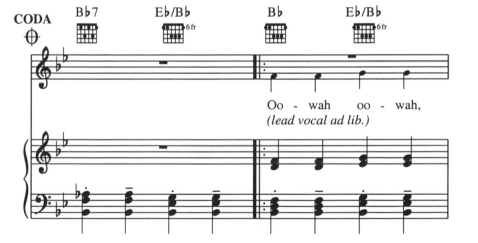

Oo - wah oo - wah,
*(lead vocal ad lib.)*

**Repeat and Fade**

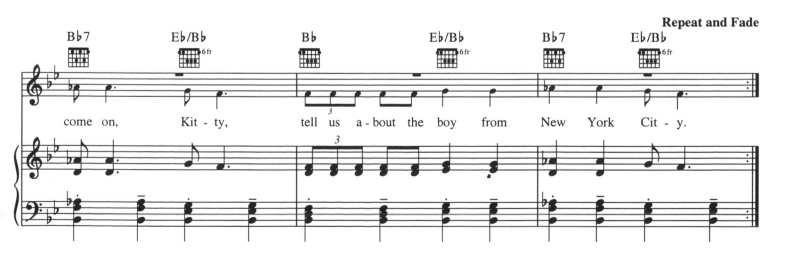

come on, Kit-ty, tell us a-bout the boy from New York Cit-y.

# BREAKFAST AT TIFFANY'S
## Theme from the Paramount Picture BREAKFAST AT TIFFANY'S

Music by
HENRY MANCINI

**Moderately, with expression**

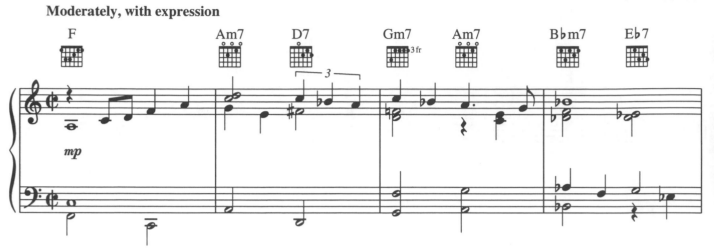

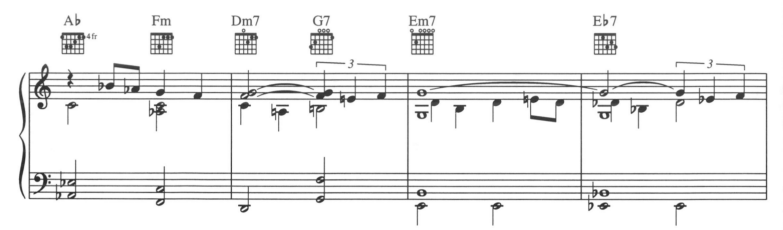

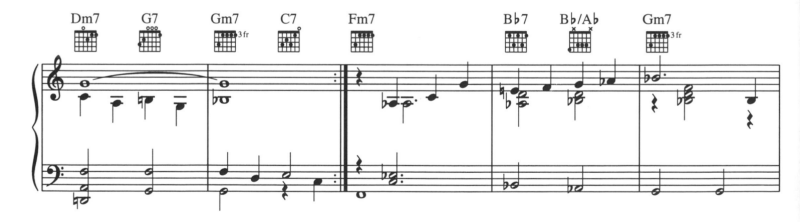

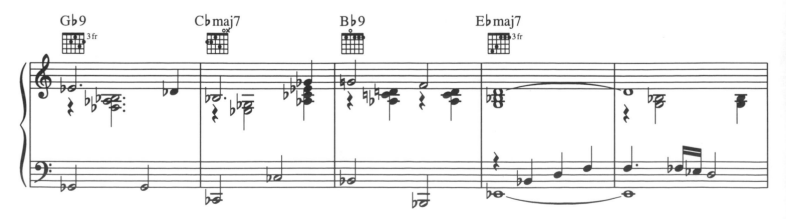

21

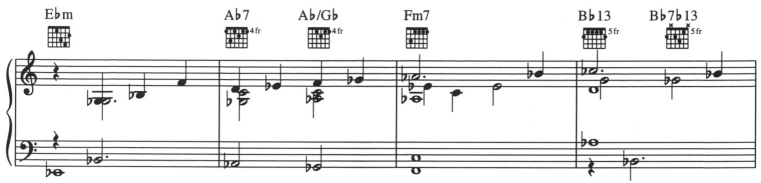

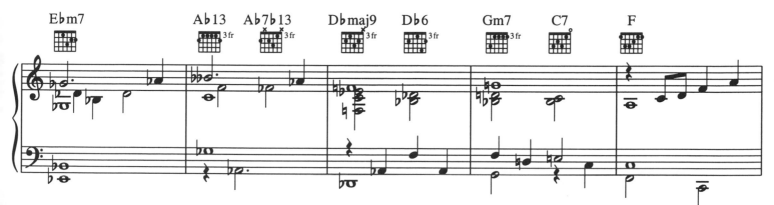

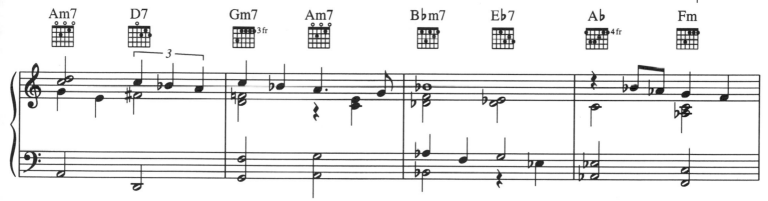

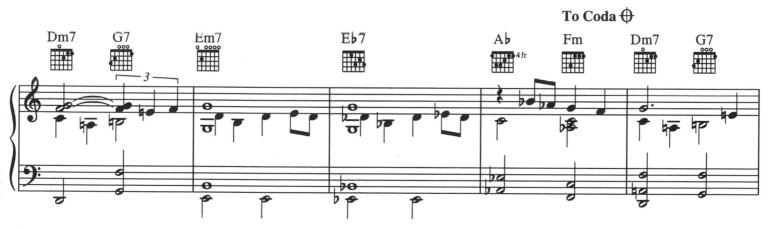

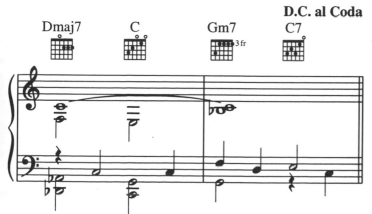

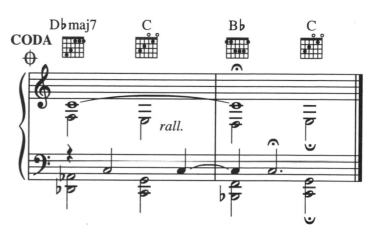

# EASTER PARADE

featured in the Motion Picture Irving Berlin's EASTER PARADE

Words and Music by
IRVING BERLIN

# EV'RY STREET'S A BOULEVARD
## (In Old New York)
### from HAZEL FLAG

Words by BOB HILLIARD
Music by JULE STYNE

# FORTY-FIVE MINUTES FROM BROADWAY

Words and Music by
GEORGE M. COHAN

Tempo di Valse.

you want to see the real jay del - e - ga tion, The place where the
tell them old jokes and they laugh till they sick - en; There's gig - gles and

real ru - bens dwell, _____ Just hop on a train at the
grins here to let. _____ I told them that one a - bout

Grand Cen - tral Sta tion, Get off when they shout "New Ro - chelle." _____
"Why does a chick - en" The ru - bens are all laugh - ing yet. _____

CHORUS.

On - ly for - ty-five minutes from Broad - way, think of the changes it
On - ly for - ty-five minutes from Broad - way, not a ca - fé in the

# FORTY SECOND STREET

Words by AL DUBIN
Music by HARRY WARREN

sex - y la - dies from the Eight-ies, who are in - dis - creet._____ They're

side by side,_____ they're glo - ri - fied_____ where the

un - der - world can meet the e - lite,___ For - ty Sec - ond Street.

naught-y, bawd-y, gawd-y, sport-y, For - ty Sec-ond Street.

# GIVE ME YOUR TIRED, YOUR POOR

## from the Stage Production MISS LIBERTY

Words by EMMA LAZARUS
From the Poem "The New Colossus"
Music by IRVING BERLIN

# GOD BLESS AMERICA

Words and Music by
IRVING BERLIN

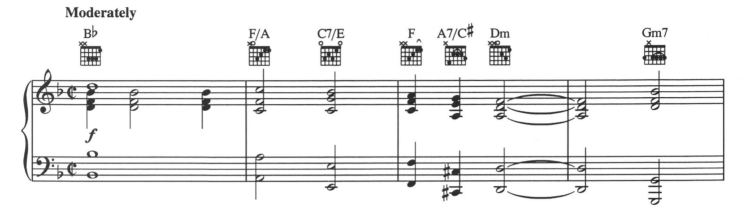

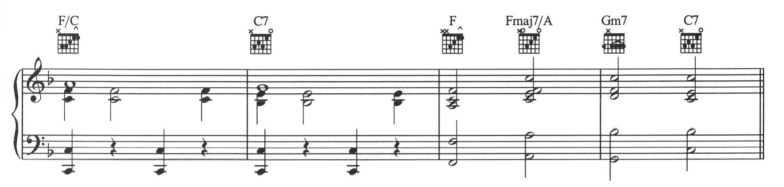

While the storm clouds gath - er    far a - cross the

sea,    let us swear al - le - giance

to a land that's free. Let us all be

grate - ful for a land so fair,

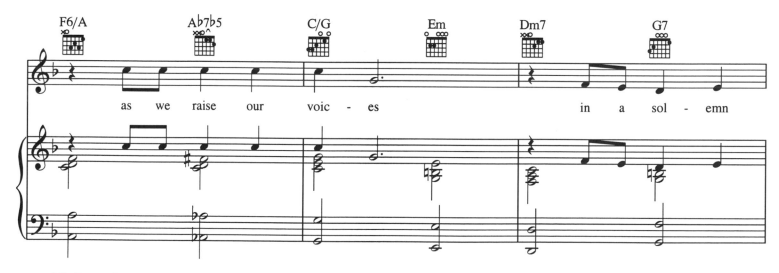

as we raise our voic - es in a sol - emn

**Moderately**

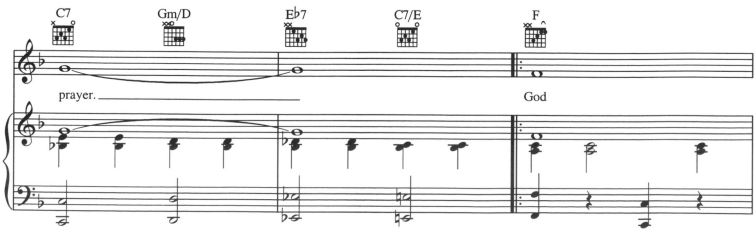

prayer._____ God

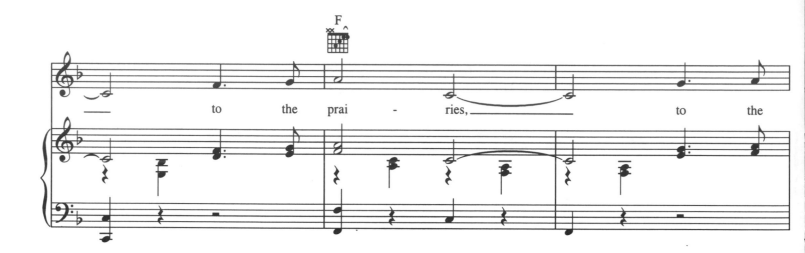

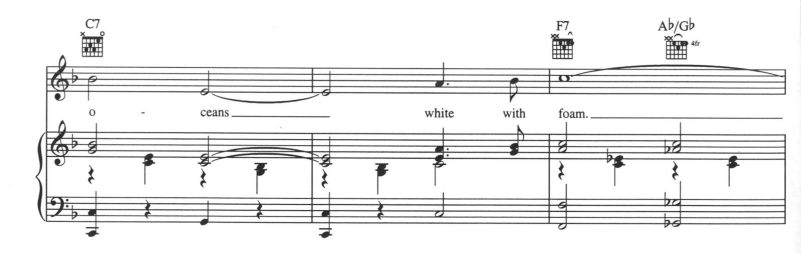

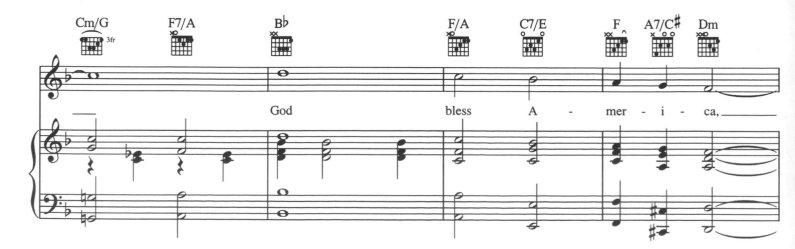

45

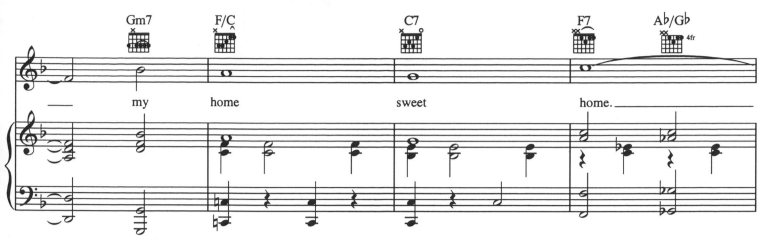

my home sweet home.

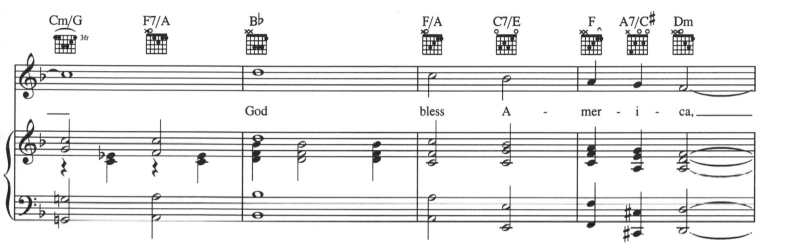

God bless A - mer - i - ca,

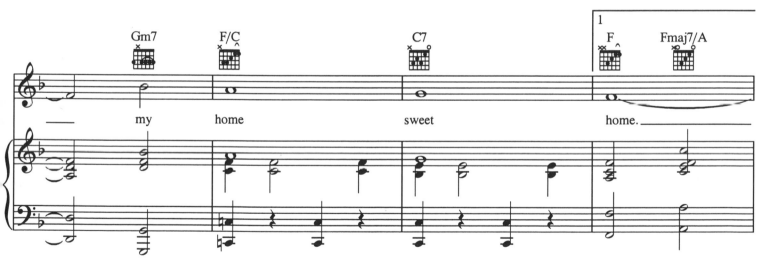

my home sweet home.

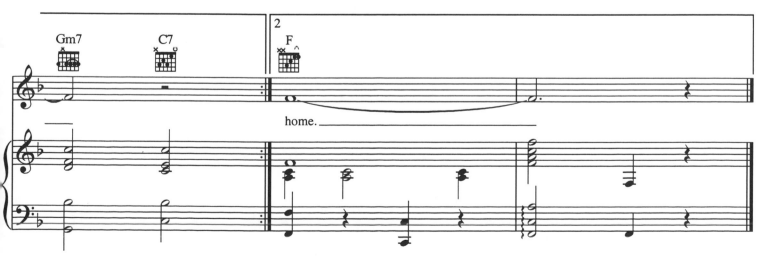

home.

# GIVE MY REGARDS TO BROADWAY

Words and Music by
GEORGE M. COHAN

start      for      Old      New      York      once      more? _____ With __
smile      and      charge      it      up      to      me; _____ Men - tion

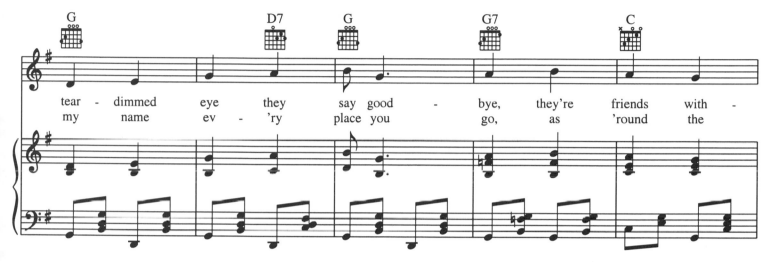

tear - dimmed      eye      they      say      good - bye,      they're      friends      with -
my      name      ev - 'ry      place      you      go,      as      'round      with      the

out      a      doubt; _____ when      the      man      on      the      pier
town      you      roam. _____ Wish      you'd      call      on      my      gal,      Now      re -

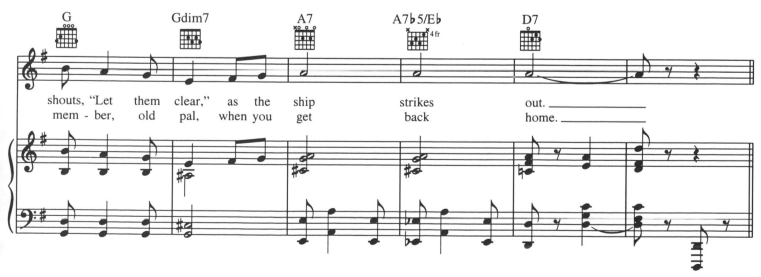

shouts, "Let      them      clear,"      as      the      ship      strikes      out. _____
mem - ber,      old      pal,      when      you      get      back      home. _____

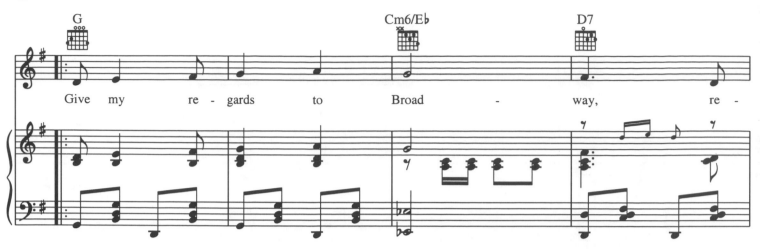

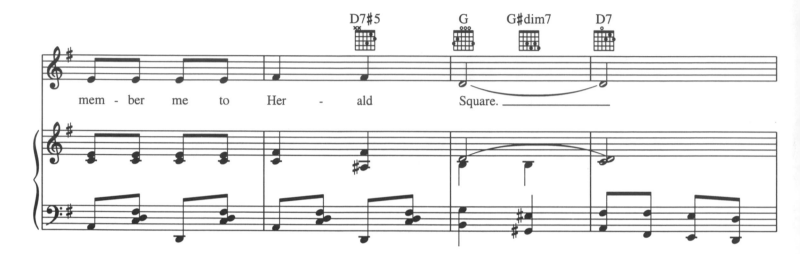

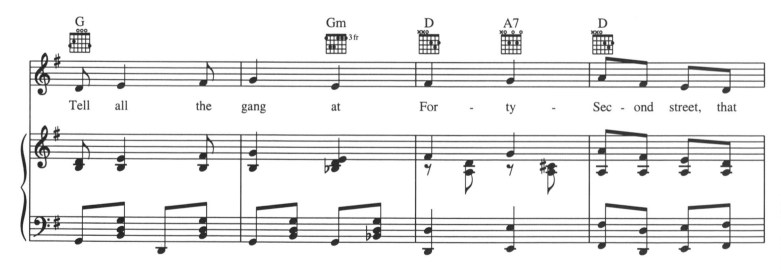

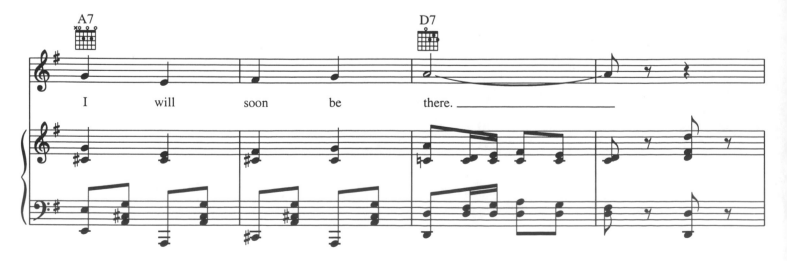

Whis - per of how I'm yearn - ing, to

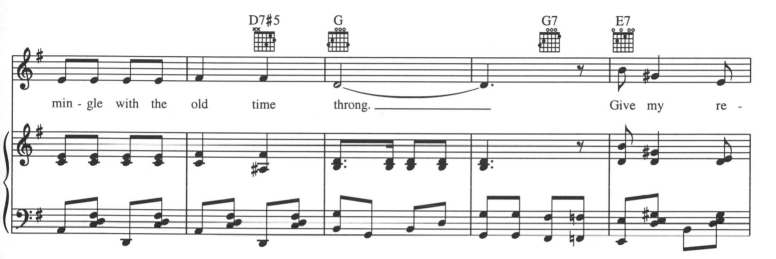

min - gle with the old time throng. _____ Give my re -

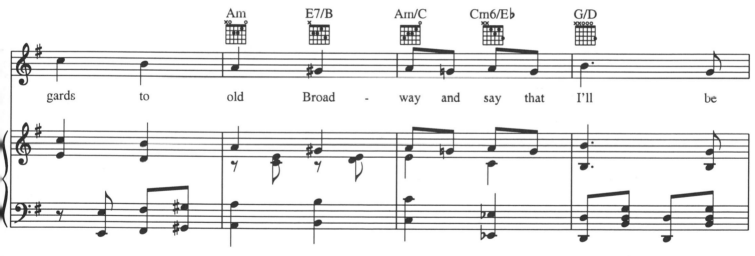

gards to old Broad - way and say that I'll be

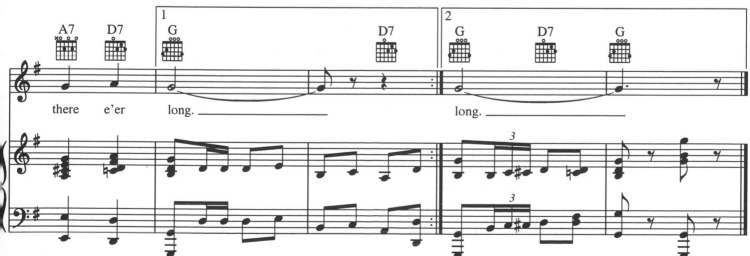

there e'er long. _____    long. _____

# HARLEM NOCTURNE

Music by EARLE HAGEN
Words by DICK ROGERS

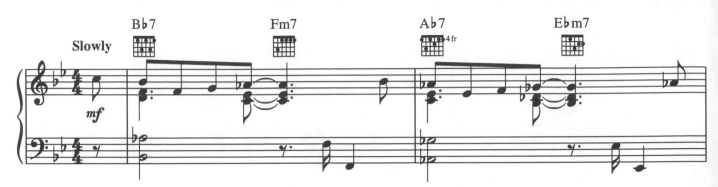

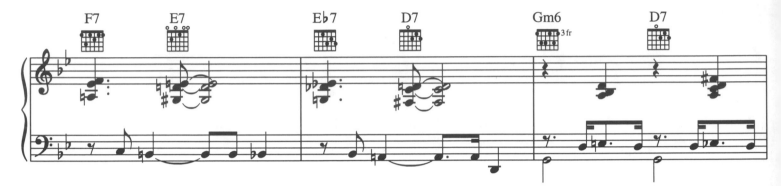

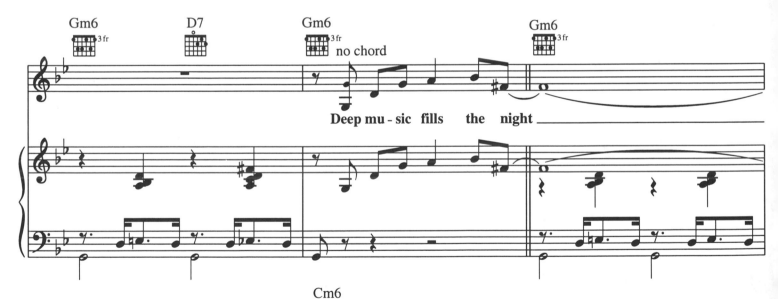

# IT'S CHRISTMAS IN NEW YORK

Words and Music by
BILLY BUTT

# I LOVE NEW YORK

Words and Music by
STEVE KARMEN

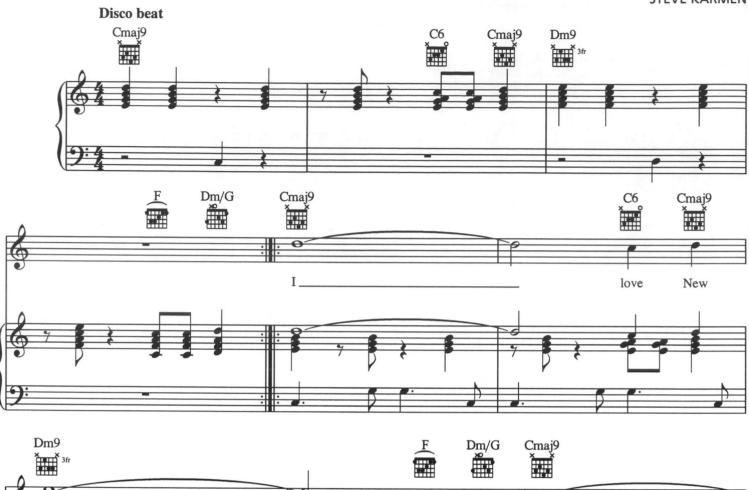

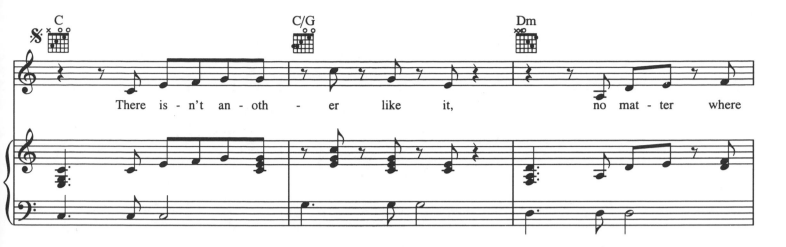

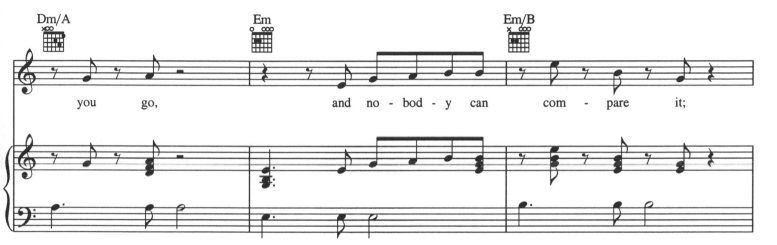

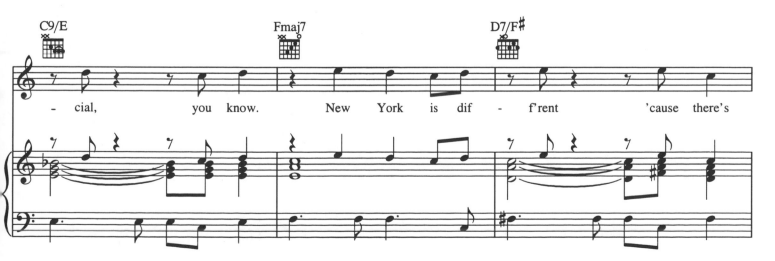

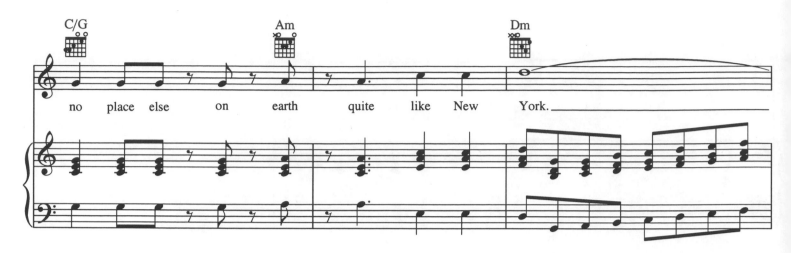

no place else on earth quite like New York._____

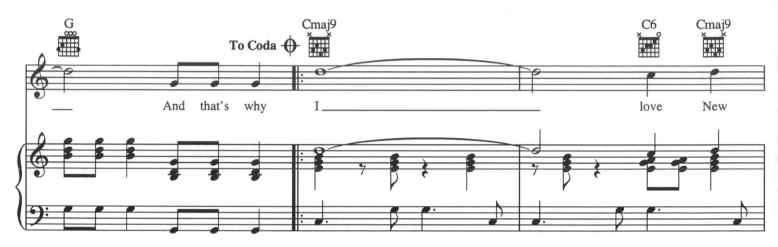

And that's why I_____ love New

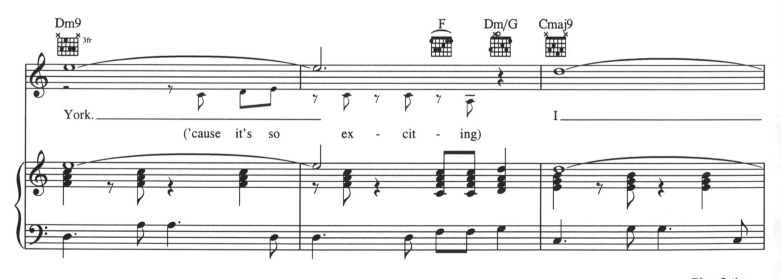

York._____ ('cause it's so ex - cit - ing) I_____

**Play 3 times**

love New York._____ (and there's no place like it)

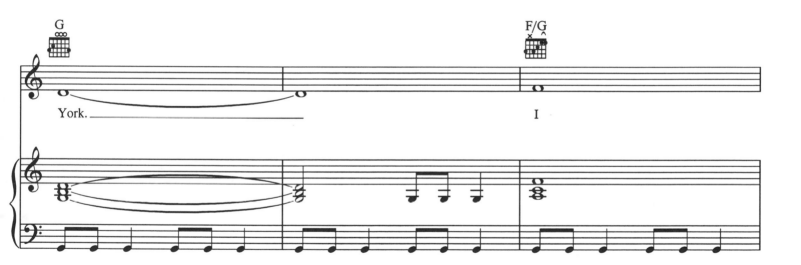

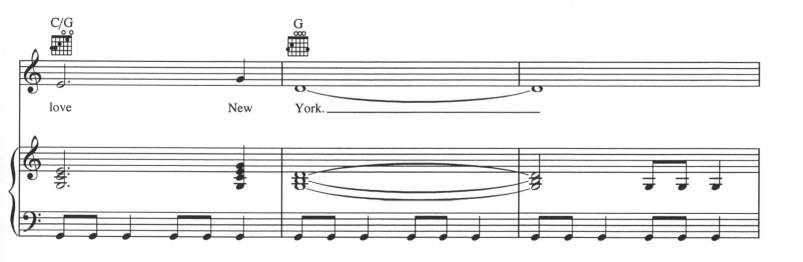

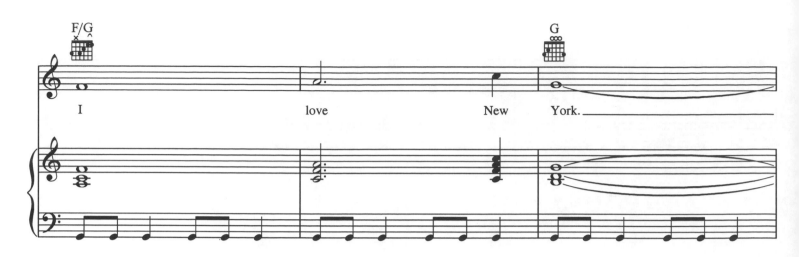

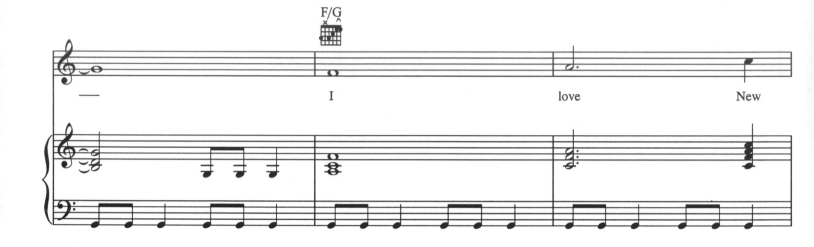

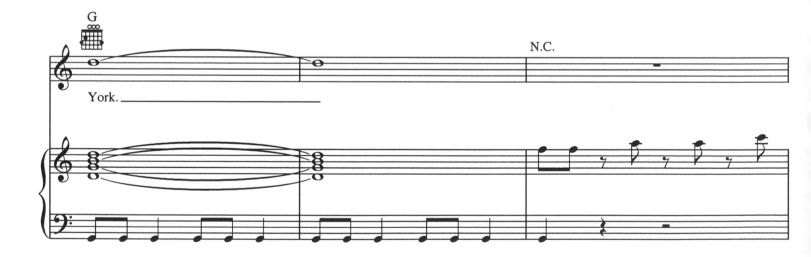

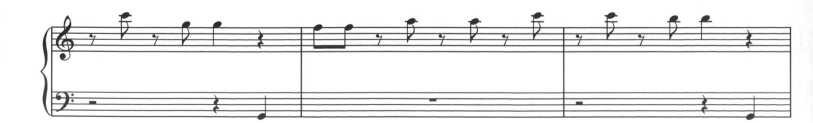

**D.S. al Coda**

**CODA**

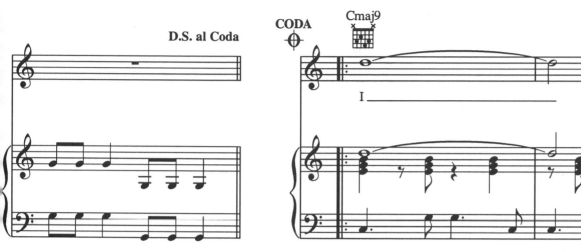

I _____ love New

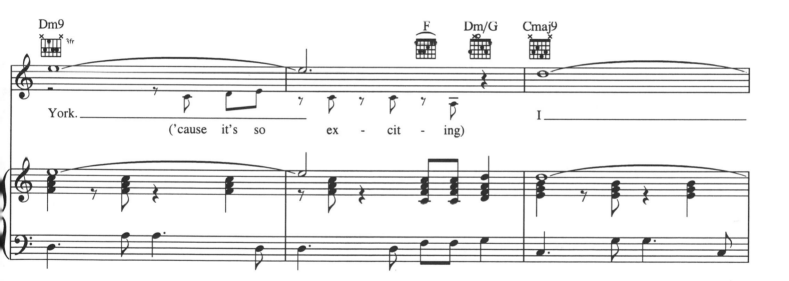

York._____ ('cause it's so ex - cit - ing) I _____

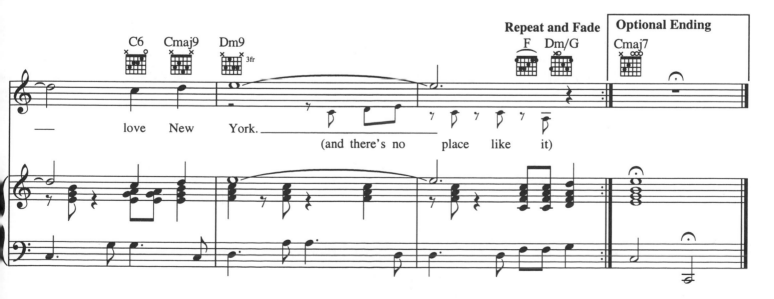

— love New York._____ (and there's no place like it)

# ISLE OF HOPE, ISLE OF TEARS

## Recorded by The Irish Tenors

Words and Music by
BRENDAN GRAHAM

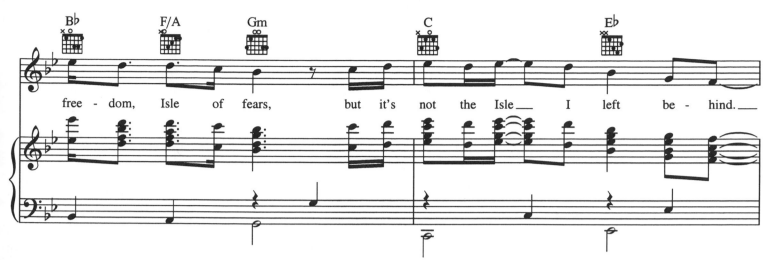

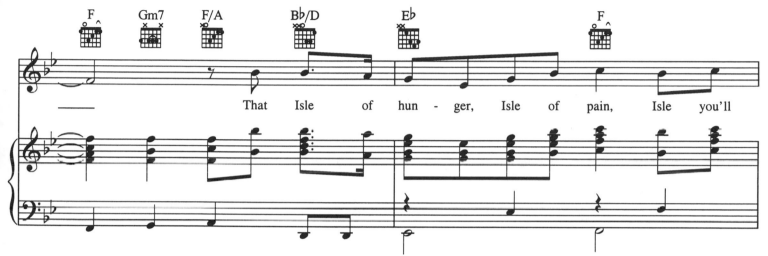

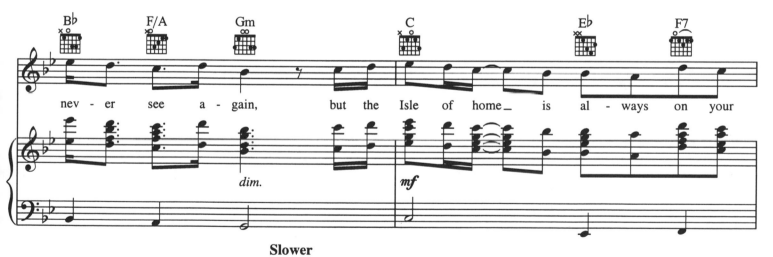

**Slower**

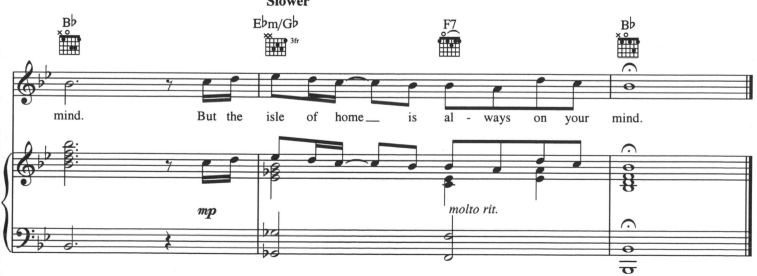

# LULLABY OF BROADWAY

Words by AL DUBIN
Music by HARRY WARREN

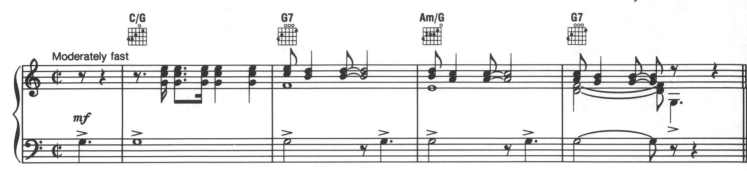

Come on a-long and lis-ten to____ the lul - la - by of Broad - way.

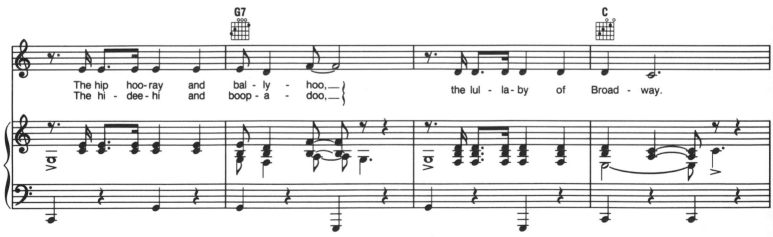

The hip hoo-ray and bal - ly - hoo,____ the lul - la - by of Broad - way.
The hi - dee - hi and boop - a - doo,____

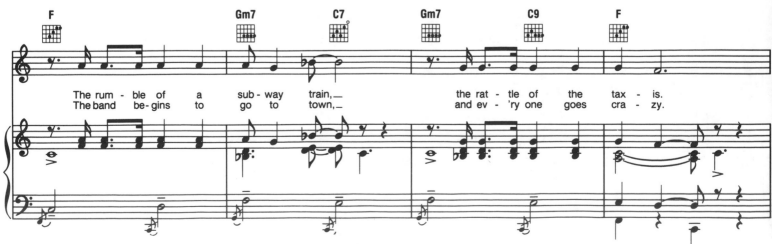

The rum - ble of a sub - way train,____ the rat - tle of the tax - is.
The band be - gins to go to town,____ and ev - 'ry one goes cra - zy.

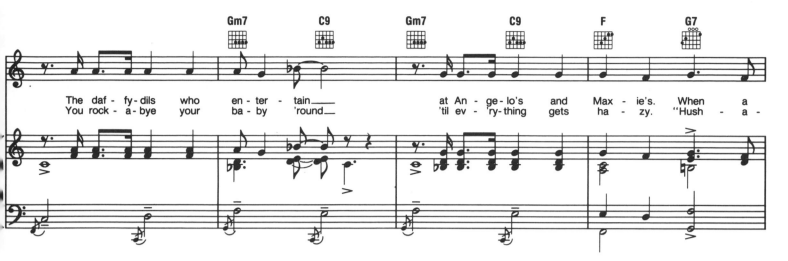

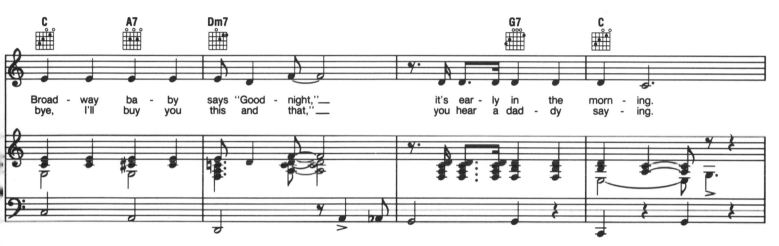

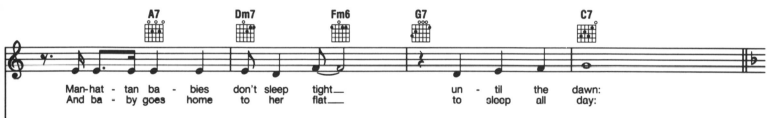

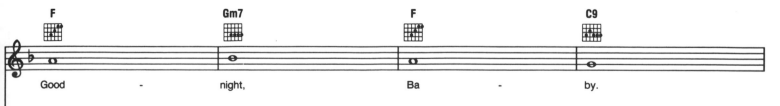

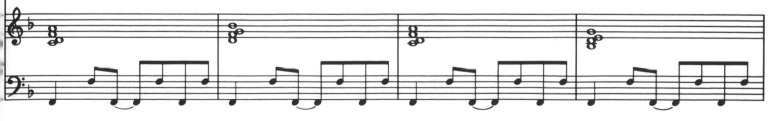

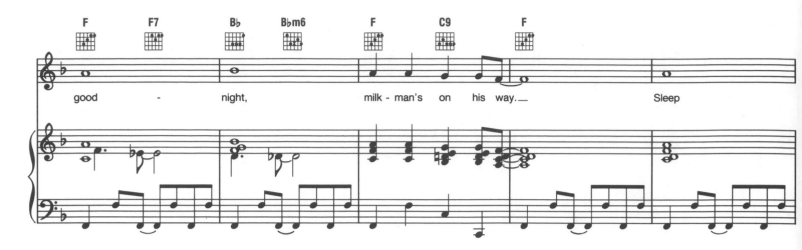

good - night, milk - man's on his way.___ Sleep

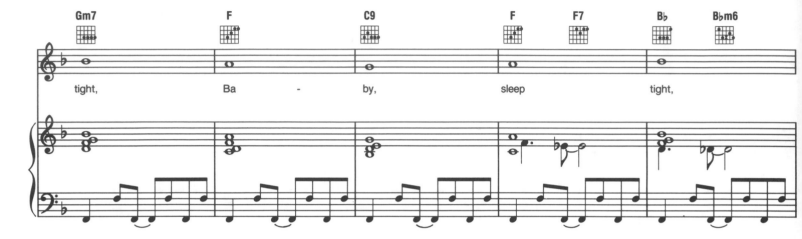

tight, Ba - by, sleep tight,

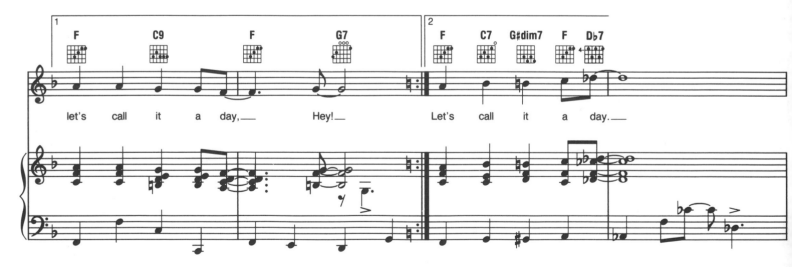

let's call it a day,___ Hey!___ Let's call it a day.___

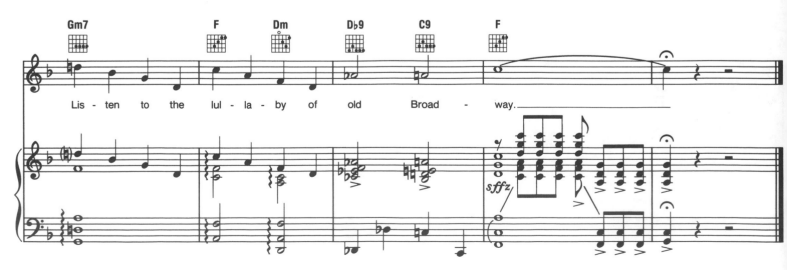

Lis - ten to the lul - la - by of old Broad - way.___

# N.Y.C.
## from the Musical Production ANNIE

Lyric by MARTIN CHARNIN
Music by CHARLES STROUSE

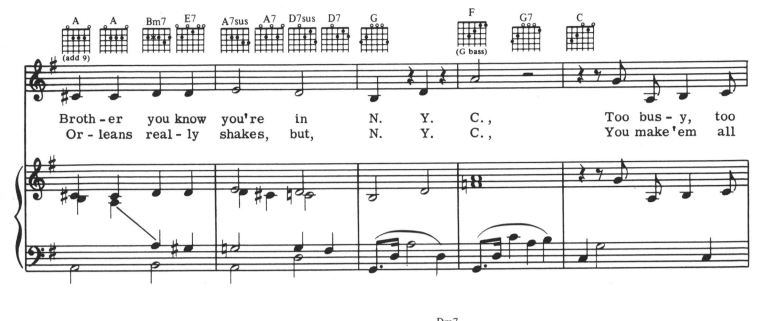

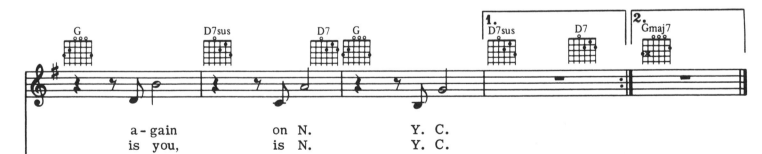

# MANHATTAN
### from the Broadway Musical THE GARRICK GAIETIES

Words by LORENZ HART
Music by RICHARD RODGERS

We'll set - tle down right here in town.

We'll have Man-hat - tan | The Bronx and Stat - en Is - land too; \_\_\_\_\_ It's love - ly
We'll go to Green-wich | Where mod - ern men itch to be free; \_\_\_\_\_ And Bowl - ing
We'll go to Yonk - ers | Where true love con - quers in the wilds; \_\_\_\_\_ And starve to -
We'll have Man-hat - tan | The Bronx and Stat - en Is - land too; \_\_\_\_\_ We'll try to

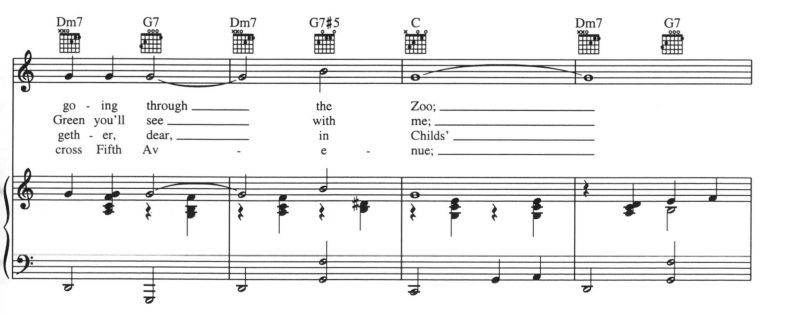

go - ing through \_\_\_\_\_ the Zoo; \_\_\_\_\_
Green you'll see \_\_\_\_\_ with me; \_\_\_\_\_
geth - er, dear, \_\_\_\_\_ in Childs' \_\_\_\_\_
cross Fifth Av - e - nue; \_\_\_\_\_

It's ver - y fan - cy / On old De - lan - cey / Street, you know; _____ / The sub - way
We'll bathe at Bright - on / The fist you'll fright - en / When you're in; _____ / Your bath - ing
We'll go to Cone - y / And eat bo - log - ny on a roll; _____ / In Cen - tral
As black as on - yx / We'll find the Bron - nix / Park Ex - press; _____ / Our Flat - bush

charms us so, _____ When balm - y breez - es blow / To and fro; / And tell me what street
suit so thin _____ Will make the shell - fish grin / Fin to fin; / I'd like to take a
Park, we'll stroll _____ Where our first kiss we stole, / Soul to soul; / And for some high fare
flat, I guess _____ Will be a great suc - cess. / More or less; / A short va - ca - tion

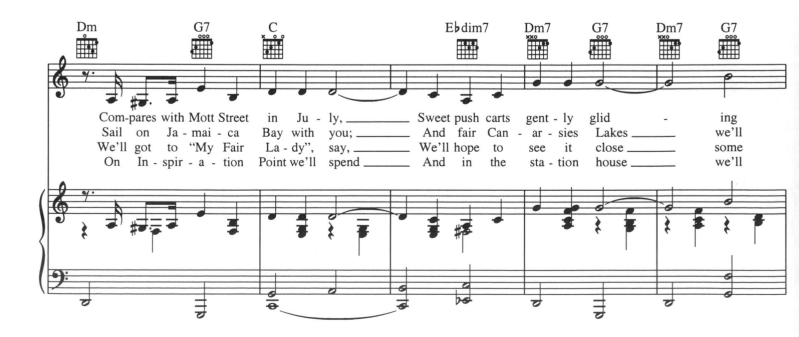

Com - pares with Mott Street in Ju - ly, _____ Sweet push carts gent - ly glid - ing
Sail on Ja - mai - ca Bay with you; _____ And fair Can - ar - sies Lakes _____ we'll
We'll got to "My Fair La - dy", say, _____ We'll hope to see it close _____ some
On In - spir - a - tion Point we'll spend / And in the sta - tion house _____ we'll

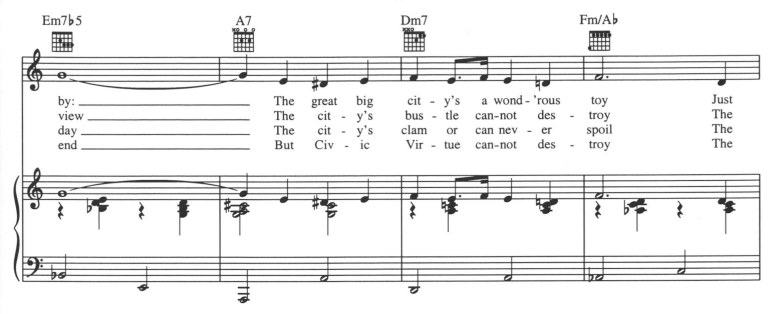

by: _____ The great big cit - y's a wond - 'rous toy Just
view _____ The cit - y's bus - tle can-not des - troy The
day _____ The cit - y's clam - or can nev - er spoil The
end _____ But Civ - ic Vir - tue can-not des - troy The

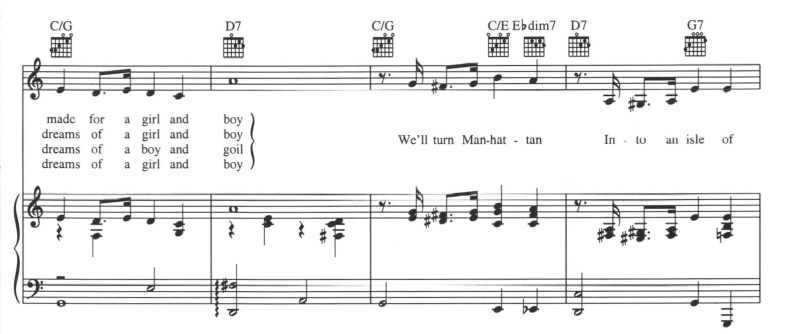

made for a girl and boy
dreams of a girl and boy
dreams of a boy and goil
dreams of a girl and boy

We'll turn Man-hat - tan      In - to an isle of

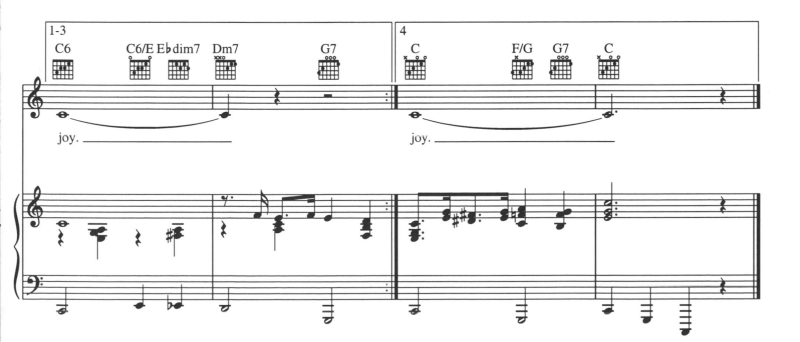

joy. _____

joy. _____

# THEME FROM "NEW YORK, NEW YORK"

Music by JOHN KANDER
Words by FRED EBB

shoes  are  long - ing  to  stray

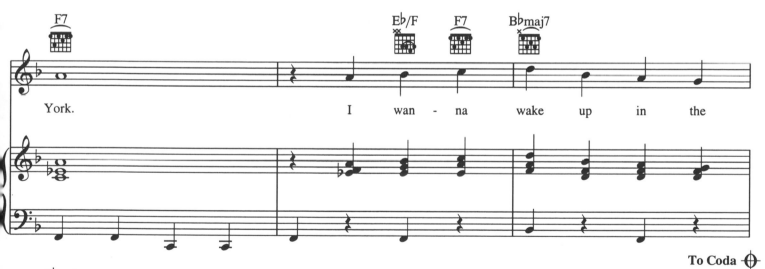

and  step  a - round  the  heart __ of  it,

(D.S.) *Instrumental*

New  York,  New

York.  I  wan - na  wake  up  in  the

**To Coda** ✛

cit - y  that  does - n't  sleep

to  find  I'm

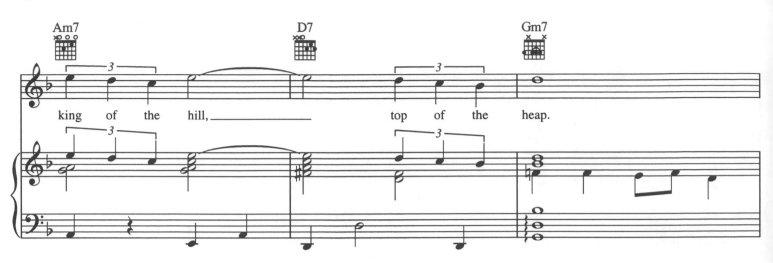

king of the hill, _____ top of the heap.

My lit - tle town blues are melt - ing a -

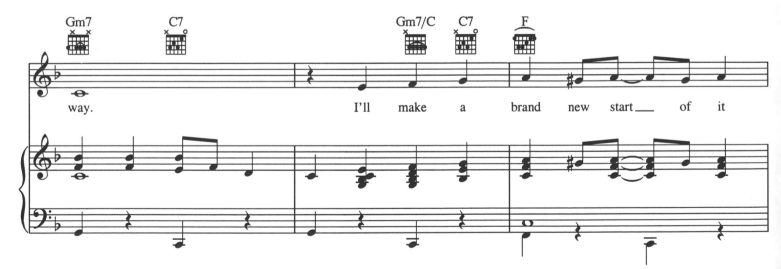

way. I'll make a brand new start__ of it

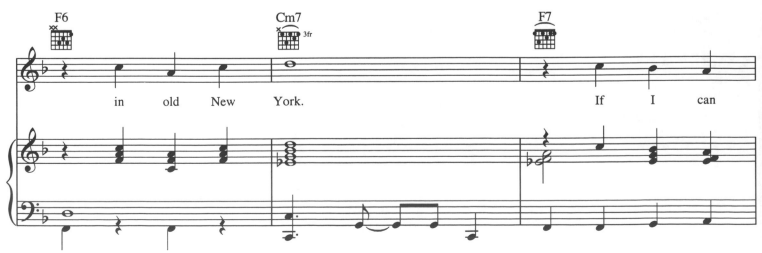

in old New York. If I can

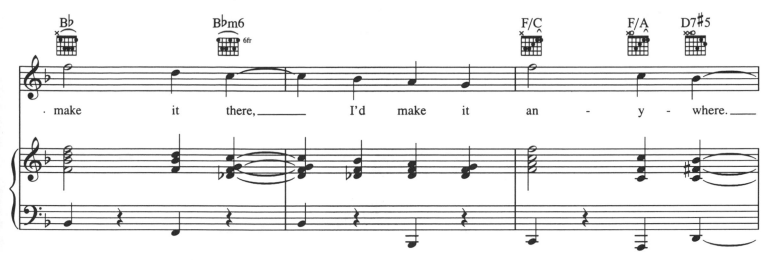

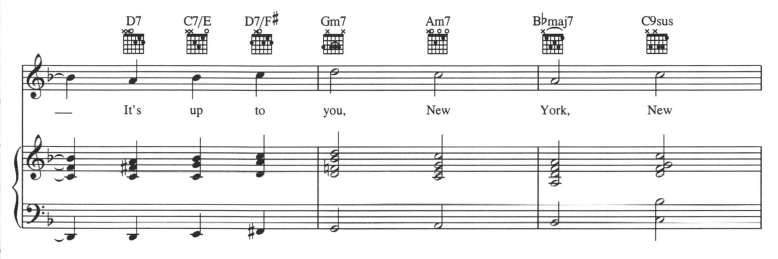

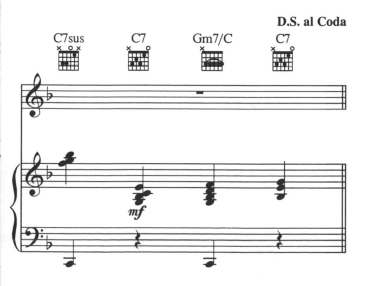

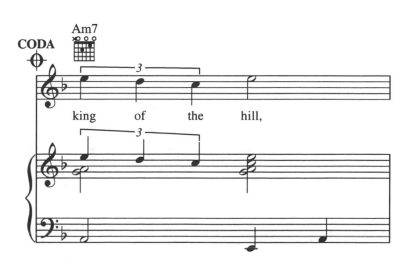

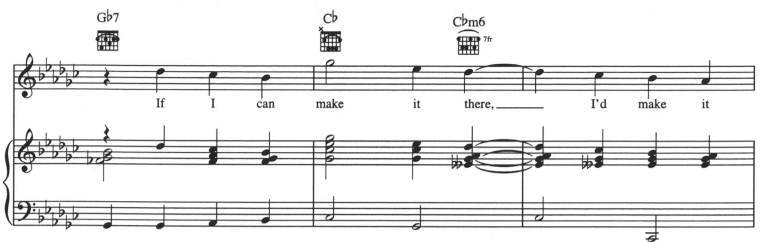

If I can make it there, _____ I'd make it

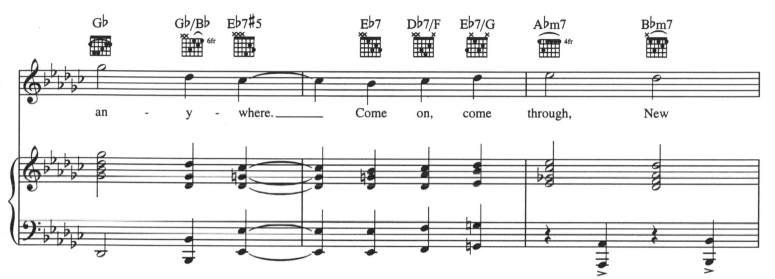

an - y - where. _____ Come on, come through, New

York, New York. _____

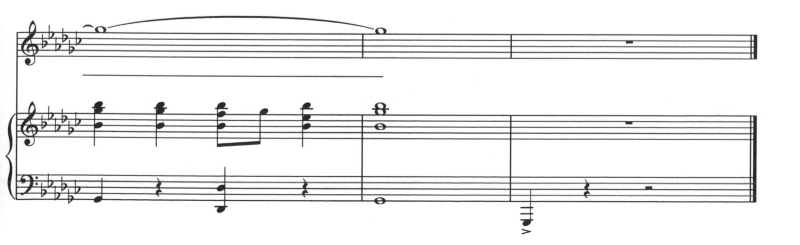

# NEW YORK STATE OF MIND

Words and Music by
BILLY JOEL

**Slowly, with a Blues feel**

1. Some folks___ like to get a - way take a
2. I've seen___ all the mov - ie stars in their
3., 5. Comes down___ to re - al - i - ty and it's
4. *Instrumental*

hol - i - day from the neigh - bor - hood, hop a flight to Mi -
fan - cy cars and their lim - ou - sines, been high in the
fine with me, 'cause I've let it slide. Don't care if it's

am - i Beach or to Hol - ly - wood.
Rock - ies___ un - der the ev - er - greens.
Chi - na - town or on Riv - er - side.

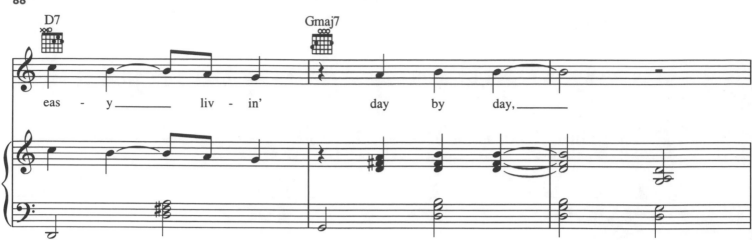

eas - y_____ liv - in' day by day,_____

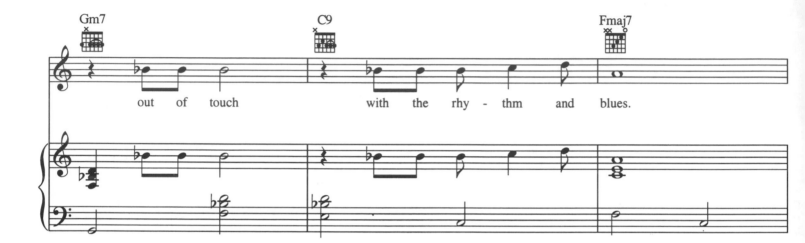

out of touch with the rhy - thm and blues.

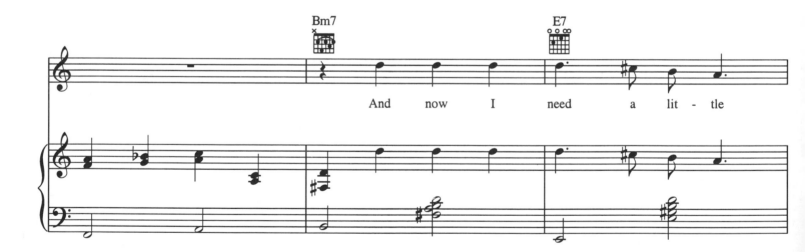

And now I need a lit - tle

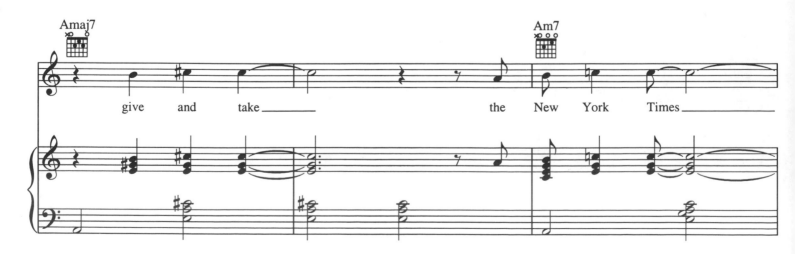

give and take_____ the New York Times_____

the Dai - ly News._____

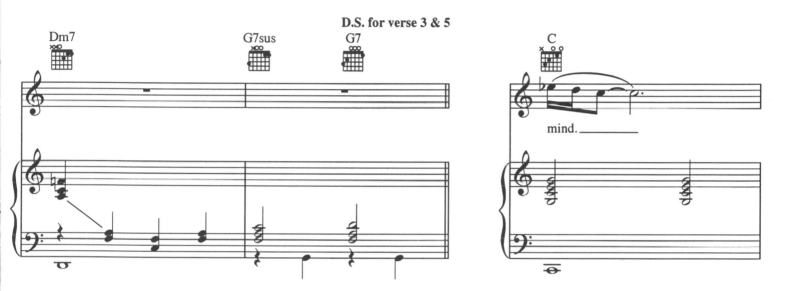

**D.S. for verse 3 & 5**

mind._____

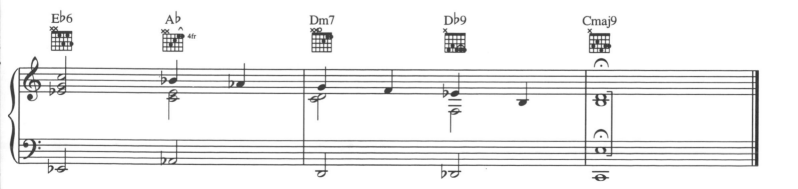

# ON BROADWAY

Words and Music by BARRY MANN, CYNTHIA WEIL,
MIKE STOLLER and JERRY LEIBER

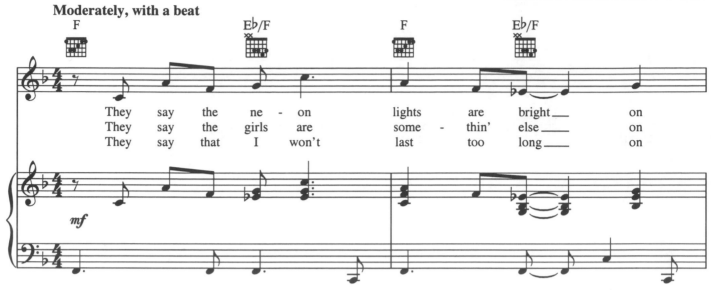

They say the ne - on lights are bright____ on
They say the girls are some - thin' else____ on
They say that I won't last too long____ on

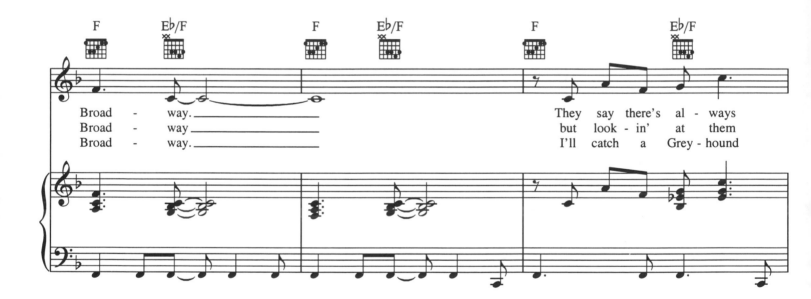

Broad - way._____ They say there's al - ways
Broad - way_____ but look - in' at them
Broad - way._____ I'll catch a Grey - hound

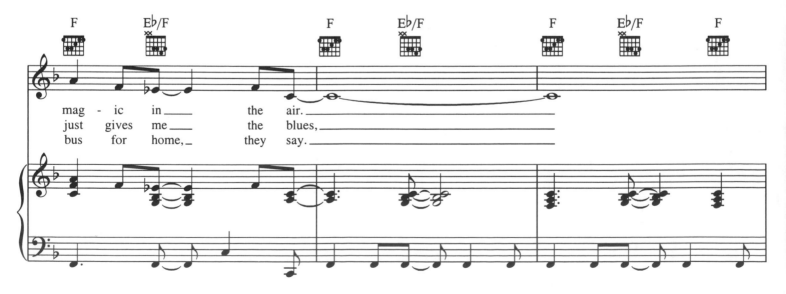

mag - ic in____ the air._____
just gives me____ the blues,_____
bus for home,____ they say._____

# TAKE THE "A" TRAIN

Words and Music by
BILLY STRAYHORN

# MORE INSPIRATIONAL
# SONGBOOKS FROM HAL LEONARD

## GOD BLESS AMERICA®
FOR THE BENEFIT OF THE TWIN TOWERS FUND
This special matching folio features 15 inspiring patriotic songs performed by top artists. Includes: Amazing Grace (Tramaine Hawkins) ★ America the Beautiful (Frank Sinatra) ★ Blowin' in the Wind (Bob Dylan) ★ Bridge over Troubled Water (Simon & Garfunkel) ★ Coming Out of the Dark (Gloria Estefan) ★ God Bless America® (Celine Dion) ★ God Bless the U.S.A. (Lee Greenwood) ★ Hero (Mariah Carey) ★ Land of Hope and Dreams (Bruce Springsteen and the E Street Band) ★ Lean on Me (Bill Withers) ★ Peaceful World (John Mellencamp) ★ The Star Spangled Banner (The Mormon Tabernacle Choir) ★ There's a Hero (Billy Gilman) ★ This Land Is Your Land (Peter Seeger) ★ We Shall Overcome (Mahalia Jackson).

_____00313196 Piano/Vocal/Guitar............$16.95

IRVING BERLIN'S
## GOD BLESS AMERICA® & OTHER SONGS
## FOR A BETTER NATION
This songbook features 35 songs to unite all Americans: Abraham, Martin and John ★ Amazing Grace ★ America ★ America the Beautiful ★ Battle Hymn of the Republic ★ Everything Is Beautiful ★ From a Distance ★ God Bless America® ★ God of Our Fathers ★ He Ain't Heavy...He's My Brother ★ I Believe ★ If I Had a Hammer ★ Imagine ★ Last Night I Had the Strangest Dream ★ Let Freedom Ring ★ Let There Be Peace on Earth ★ The Lord's Prayer ★ My Country 'Tis of Thee (America) ★ Pray for Our Nation ★ Precious Lord, Take My Hand ★ The Star Spangled Banner ★ Stars and Stripes Forever ★ This Is a Great Country ★ This Is My Country ★ This Land Is Your Land ★ United We Stand ★ We Shall Overcome ★ What a Wonderful World ★ What the World Needs Now Is Love ★ You'll Never Walk Alone ★ You're a Grand Old Flag ★ and more.

_____00310825 Piano/Vocal/Guitar............$12.95

## FORTY SONGS FOR A BETTER WORLD
40 songs with a message, including: All You Need Is Love ★ Blackbird ★ Bless the Beasts and Children ★ Candle on the Water ★ Child of Mine ★ Circle of Life ★ Colors of the Wind ★ Count Your Blessings Instead of Sheep ★ Ebony and Ivory ★ Everything Is Beautiful ★ The Flower That Shattered the Stone ★ Friends ★ From a Distance ★ God Bless the U.S.A. ★ Gonna Build a Mountain ★ He Ain't Heavy...He's My Brother ★ I Am Your Child ★ I Believe ★ If I Had a Hammer (The Hammer Song) ★ If I Ruled the World ★ If We Only Have Love (Quand on N'a Que L'amour) ★ Imagine ★ The Impossible Dream (The Quest) ★ In Harmony ★ Let's Get Together ★ Lost in the Stars ★ Love Can Build a Bridge ★ Love in Any Language ★ Make Your Own Kind of Music ★ One Song ★ Ordinary Miracles ★ The Rainbow Connection ★ Tears in Heaven ★ Turn! Turn! Turn! (To Everything There Is a Season) ★ What a Wonderful World ★ What the World Needs Now Is Love ★ With a Little Help from My Friends ★ You'll Never Walk Alone ★ You've Got a Friend ★ You've Got to Be Carefully Taught.

_____00310096 Piano/Vocal/Guitar............$15.95

## LET FREEDOM RING!
*The Phillip Keveren Series*
15 favorites celebrating the land of the free, including: America, the Beautiful ★ Anchors Aweigh ★ Battle Hymn of the Republic ★ Eternal Father, Strong to Save ★ God Bless Our Native Land ★ God of Our Fathers ★ My Country, 'Tis of Thee (America) ★ Semper Fidelis ★ The Star Spangled Banner ★ Stars and Stripes Forever ★ Washington Post March ★ Yankee Doodle ★ Yankee Doodle Boy ★ You're a Grand Old Flag.

_____00310839 Piano Solo............$9.95

FOR MORE INFORMATION, SEE YOUR LOCAL MUSIC DEALER,
OR WRITE TO:

HAL•LEONARD®
CORPORATION
7777 W. BLUEMOUND RD. P.O. BOX 13819 MILWAUKEE, WI 53213

Visit Hal Leonard Online at
**www.halleonard.com**